For Kimsy,
the bravest and the most beautiful
Princess in all the world.

I spend my days in many different ways,
but every day I try to help her smile.

To all of the 'Amazing Angels' at the Alexandra Hospital in Cheadle, Stockport, including all front of house/administration staff, those who ensure everything runs smoothly, and who set the relaxed ambience of an amazing hospital.

My gratitude could never be fully repaid for all you have done for my wife Kimberly May Roberts. Thank you for your humanity, your courage, and your compassion. Such wonderful people.

I really struggle to put into words how much you all mean to me. It puts a lump in my throat when I think of all you have done to help save the life of the one I love. I am truly humbled by your dedication, your skills, and willingness to help. I am forever in debt to you all. Thank you for being there for Kim, and for us.

Colorectal Surgeon
Mr Mo Saeed

Richmond Ward
Carla
Debbie
Eamonn
Helen
Mirela
Nikki
Wendy

Chester Suite HDU/ICU
Agnes
Andrea
Anna
Beth
Caroline
Donna
Florence
Holly
Jessy
Josh
Karolina
Kelly
Mashid

Stoma Nurse
Donn
Kay

Oncologist
Dr Jujees Hassan

Physio
Amy
Joanna
Sarah

Lancaster Ward
Elyse
Hannah
Sara
Toni

Pharmacy
Samina

Wound Nurse
Caroline
Cherry
Emilyn
Lesley (NHS Treatment Rooms)
Rochane
Soledad

Catering
Abib
Bryony
Denise
Emma
Rob

Kimsy and I, Lusty Glaze Beach, Cornwall. July 2018.

Contents

Intro 15
Nob-ility 21
Erubescence 22
How we've grown 23
Well versed 24
Fist of Fury 25
An open story 26
Tarden view 27
Seasons change 28
A hanging 29
The Persistence of Memory 30
Don't stop 31
Platform shoes 32
Rain 33
Travelling wife 34
2-minute beach clean 35
Open water 36
Sans Syrup 37
Hair, bear bunch 38
Panic room 39
In hope we trust 40
Clowder 41
Dare to be you 42
Gist 43
Sales Force 44
Public observer 45
Corduroy 46
Bored of the flies 47
Nephrologist's muse 48
Flower power 49
Unity 50
Pay and display 51

Proboscis	52
Quite Frank, Poetry	53
Smiggles' regulars	54
Fridge Fairy	55
A bag, for life.	56
Is my PA on leave?	58
Amazing Angels	60
Mr Overall	61
Sea me	62
Puppy love	63
On we go	64
For what?	65
To the end	66
Fruity	67
Fortune Teller	68
Matey	69
Super Cub	70
Class clown	71
Paradise found	72
Johns	73
Write you	74
Help the aged	75
Supermarket Steve	76
Christmas Eve	78
Vermin	79
I don't like	80
Grifter	82
A journey North	83
Get real	85
Mistakes	86
Unwanted; the penchant of tension	87
Offended	88
Dreams of summer	89

She/Her	90
Marie de' Medici Cycle	91
I love her	92
Crazy Town	94
What horror	95
Wide awake club	96
Dali's Meadow	97
Travelling man	98
Snow day	99
Woman Hitler	100
Struggle	101
Telescopic	102
0.000002%	103
Revolting	104
Mooning	105
Night sky	106
Cheshire illuminations	107
Hoot	108
The last days of summer	109
Top shelf	110
Antiques Roadshow	111
Wet	112
A summer of discontent	113
Dance with me	114
The painting	116
Dinner for two	117
Forever yours	118
Days of wonder	119
Chai	120
Tea and Toast	121
An ode to the modern-day Suffragette	122
Street life	123
The Darkness	124

The Northern Water 125
New day 126
Chance 127
Best Man 128
Poems 129
Epilogue 130

Intro

I am a lot of things, but an International Gigolo certainly isn't one of them. Therefore, I would like to take this opportunity to apologise in advance if you purchased this book with the expectancy of erotic tales and hedonistic 'Mills and Boon' type adventure. I'm very sorry, but this book has a more 'Pam Ayres on glue' type feel to it.

The book title/cover is purely tongue in cheek (*no pun intended*). You see there are rumours, (*I might have started them*) that in my prime I was a mainstay on the International Gigolo Scene, and for want of a better description 'a bit of a lady's man.' However, that statement could not be any further from the truth. Now while I cannot confirm nor deny these rumours, hearsay has it that I only charged £2.50 per hour (*£2.80 in affluent areas*) for my services yet rarely managed more than a few minutes on task, leaving the rest of the hour spent doing chores for idle housewives intent on getting value for money while they watched Jeremy Kyle! Again, I cannot confirm nor deny such hearsay, although if I am truly honest, my main strengths now (*honed over many a year*) are my domestic cleanliness, pot washing efficiency, and ironing skills.

Nowadays though it seems I have been labelled as being 'a bit of Poet,' and, although I am here again with more of my poetry and pocket philosophy, I don't ever see myself as a Poet. Words, accompanied with their poetic cadence, somehow eke their way out of my tiny magic filled mind, and I just love to share them with those keen on escaping into my alternate safe space of sunshine and lollipops. You're welcome.

I feel an almost constant need to write things down, be it spur of the moment thoughts, or interesting words that I hear in conversation or discover as I read. Strange really as I despised reading and writing at school and did everything I possibly could to avoid them. Evidence of this emerged recently when I bumped into a girl/lady who I went to primary school with in the early 70s (*thank you, I know, I don't look old enough do I*) and I'd not seen her for at least forty years, her first words were "Oh my god Oggy, you were so naughty at school!" (*Thanks Michelle*).

Looking back, I don't think I was purposely naughty, I was just bored with the way we were corralled into dingy classrooms, that and the self-importance of the pompous teachers seemed to be greater than that of anyone else in the room. My resenting attitude towards school/teachers carried on all through my entire education, I was always funnier than the teachers too, and they really didn't like that!

My writing/poetry is completely self-taught, as natural, and as honest as I can be, but rest assured I have tried my absolute best for you here.

So, please enjoy this collection of words that I have pulled together this year, hopefully you might find solace, smiles, or a new favourite Poem amongst them.

Oh, and in keeping with my 'International Gigolo Services terms and conditions' I am very sorry but *"there are absolutely no refunds!"* Unless of course I have burnt your undergarments while ironing them, and yes, I will pay for those!

Nob-ility

They all scoffed at the plausibility of his nobility.
While he had indeed married a beautiful Princess
he confessed he had hardly ascended
to the upper echelons of society.
Though he argued their love was his only priority,
and as such, a sobriety
from his much-celebrated Gigolo past.

Having married a beautiful Princess, it is without any doubt that I am in fact a Prince! Charming...

Erubescence

Uncontrollable, taint
temporarily indelible
rushed flush of blush reveals,
repeals a moment's confidence
as gifted compliments send her pinkish.
Sheepish, she glows
a deft camouflage agin
matching rose received.
Smile beamed
beats skip
flattery quipped to charm
her arm
her heart,
stolen.

"Blushing is the most peculiar and most human of all expressions" - Charles Darwin.

"A friend of mine once said he likes his women like his Parmesan; strong smelling and shaved. I don't agree with that, but I don't like hairy women." - Alan Partridge.

How we've grown

Muddy urchin, ruddy faced
embraced by overbearing Nanna
squirming to avoid rogue kisses
from puckered lips with bristle banner

to lark in park, in swoop of swing
and giggled glide of slide
beamed pride of crumbling sandcastles
bread toss to pond fish topping

dragged feet opposed to shopping
to trolley seat prison with promise of lolly
a temporary folly as wail of wronged frustration
echoes, in stress of senseless scene

to moaning moody teen, a tantrum, a fandom of nothing
as bored accord of rebellion arrives to stifle
communication, inspiration, and respect
a direct result of change, of phase

oh, my days, sixteen going on twenty
knows it all, too much, plenty
yet not enough, but tuts, a lot
so bold in desperate rush to be older

schools out, forever, apron tether severed
no longer together, a childhood spent
as if lent, without rude remark of rent
thoughts and daunts of ageing rise

where, surprise goodbyes and realisation of life
steal our once impervious innocence
as crowned hands tick and sands fall,
we are appalled at how quickly we have aged.

That child is still inside us all, it is just a bit more tired, and much less enthusiastic than it once was. Just remember not to peak too early on nights out and you will be fine.

Well versed

Each a magical, come mini adventure
perhaps even a creative projection
of my rose-tinted heart,
all be it from part of my evolving story.
A frolicking foray
into a wonderland of Alice imagine
where the likes of the common pigeon
are framed and idolised,
where my love for her is reprised
throughout vast panoply of stanzas.
With candour I write for those
comatose by society, for those
undeniably joyful in sobriety
or maybe those just drunk on life.
A parity scrawled
these words for all
a call, from stall
of custodial mind.
At times with thoughts like an unmade bed
my head a DMZ for chaos.
Sometimes lost, bewildered, or overawed,
appalled by the fickle hands of time
and hurt etched by those taken.
Still, each line is curated
elated by journey, a journey shared
with words paired to moments, experiences,
and smiles. This poetry gifted
to us as we walk seemingly endless miles
in the strangest of shoes,
where we've nothing to fear
and nothing to lose, but ourselves.

Inspiration for my rhythmic ramblings comes from everywhere and anything. Poetry helps frame my thoughts and also my understanding of things. It silences doubt and irrational emotions that would otherwise be forefront in my life. Writing is an immensely powerful healer.

Fist of Fury

So, there I was, toe to toe with Tyson Fury
and what a story;
he was doing his absolute best to floor me
but I'm agile, I'm like a cat
and I told him straight "me Nan boxes better than that."
I duck and weave, I lead with a jab
one two, one two, sending
a haymaker to the side of his head
ears ringing, bringing a grimace to his face
(*even more so than usual*)
yet I admired his stubbornness and refusal to feel the pain.
Again, and again
I dodge his venomous arrows
on legs of sparrows
I'm dancing like a butterfly and stinging like Ali,
"*Yo Adrian, just look at me go,*"
I'm showboating now
playing up to the crowd
"OGGY, OGGY" sounded like "ROCKY, ROCKY,"
I've heard that chant before I thought
as he nearly caught me with a right hook to the chin.
How long has it been,
it's the sixth round and he's not even landed one punch
then, as if poetically timed,
CRUNCH, he hits me bang on the nose
and all of a sudden, he knows, he knows
he's in trouble!
Bent over double he clutches his hand
writhing in agony he can barely stand,
his hand broken, he's broken
and probs rueing the fact that he'd ever spoken
out of turn to me. "*That's what you get
for trying to jump the queue in Lidl*" I said
as little did he know the bone in my big nose
has the density of a small moon.
Anyways, the young girl Tina on the till
held my arm aloft and proclaimed me
"The heavyweight champion of Lidl,"
and I'll take that, as I only went in for a loaf.

True story.

An open story

All across the sands we schemed
where it somehow seemed we dreamed
an open story of ourselves. Where,
watched by moon and warmed by star
afar the published look-on with pride
spurred on by turn of stoic cogs
agog at whatever fun we find.
For in moments kind we celebrate
elate our inner child by skate,
of chosen path, we laugh
and find a way to live, to love.

Our fun, our laughter, our kindness, our love; these things all add to the open story that we will one day be remembered by. For now though, we can but pull from the published stories of those before us, in hope to remember them, and to learn from their adventures.

Tarden view

Cotton clouds clear
feathered kites soar
eyes tour the prize
wide morning skies reveal.
Framed,
attained through pane
vast blankets green
breathtaking scene
of model houses, of model town,
a vibrant vista gleans
fall's yellows and browns.
Vast,
ever changing mural
of soothing serenity counsel
a delight for sight
gorped effortlessly in wonder,
views plunder our hearts, content.
Lament,
as flamed sunset fires her final glow
a defiant show of searing colour,
crept cover calls
darkness falls,
and our gratitude to rest
in such picturesque paradise pondered.
Suffice to say,
we absolutely love it here.

A stay at Tarden Farm in Mellor completely captivates your senses. The ambiance and tranquility of Tarden refreshes your soul, and the surrounding countryside helps clear your mind. Such a wonderful, and incredibly beautiful place.

Thank you M & G for sharing your beautiful home with us.

Seasons change

Simplicity with a twist,
inebriating grist
of cathartic countryside's
sounds and smells.
Delights in sights,
of nature's pastels
moments wildflowers
stand like proud castles,
fortifying their meadow with colour.
Soaked in song,
leaves leap on breeze
with ease scenes please the souls
of those buoyed,
overjoyed, imbibed by surroundings
compounding peace
intoxicating senses.
Unassuming, unpretentious
autonomous in cycle, survival
in unison, an ensemble
sometimes harsh, yet so beautiful.

The simplicity, yet depth of seasons' cycle is utterly mind blowing. The resilience and beauty found within those cycles also serves as an inspiration to us all. Nature is the epitome of stoicism; it always finds a way to endure and adapt, to keep going. As should we.

A hanging

Who, in the right mind
would ever find Wood-Chip appealing!
Corners pealing
drooping ceiling,
concealing pitted walls
an Anaglypta falls to skirting.
Slow working,
pasty, never hasty, shirking
day rate decorator slurping Teas
scoffing all my biscuits with ease,
all to appease rooms vibe
and more so to comply with 'her vision,'
the almost impossible mission that is
to satisfy her eye...

While I absolutely, undeniably, and utterly detest decorating, I hate paying for a decorator more! Especially when they spend more time drinking my Tea and scoffing all my biscuits than they actually do decorating!

Oscar Wilde's last words were: "My wallpaper and I are fighting a duel to the death. One or the other of us has to go."

The Persistence of Memory

Perplexed in pants
steadfast a gasp
clicked fingered past
seemingly just a blur.
A brisk stir indeed
of moment occur
perturbed by tick and tock of clock.
Glories tasted
mind jaded
memories traded
perhaps to nothing, *niente*.
Accepting gracefully
or by rude lament
with resent
of opportunities wasted.
Yet content within the entirety
of experiences shared
for loved ones cared,
all terribly torn when time is called.
And time, time will wash away those tears.

One day you will stand in your own truth, soaked in the absolute realisation of all the things that you have seen, shared, heard, and felt. So, leave no stone unturned, as that moment of content is all that which you can take with you.

'The Persistence of Memory' is a painting by Salvador Dali from 1931.

Don't stop

Trickled source
water's fall
cascading flow
of mighty force
of roar
through tor
to Sea
to Port
in swell
in current fought
eroding path by course
without pause
snaked glinting gleam to shores
all yours
and mine to enjoy,
oh buoy!

"Don't stop, isn't it funny how you shine..." – Ian Brown/John Squire.

Platform shoes

Wild gait of frenzied Friesian
a tad sweaty and breathless to say
(just imagine a Pug in a greenhouse
on a sweltering hot summers day.)

With screaming shin splints sewn from shoes
never meant for track and field
like the easy peel of satsuma coat
skin tore effortlessly from her heels.

And to the amusement of those seated
under guard's whistle doors begin
their slow deliberate synchronicity of slide
to stop late comers getting in.

Forlorn, resigned to platform mime
of mouthed words and thrown hand gesture
livid beyond all reason because
of early diesel pig departure!

There is always something oddly amusing about that one person running for a train (or bus). Although, unlike the majority of passengers already aboard, I personally am always rooting for that last struggling straggler to make it, especially if said train has departed a bit earlier than scheduled.

<u>However,</u> watching them mouth words and gesture emphatically towards the train as it pulls away without them is absolutely priceless, and even funnier if it is on a Monday morning, and it is raining.

Rain

White forks crack open
the aphotic inked dark sky
clapped clash of raging clouds all thrive
in relentless stair rod reign
rapped slashed tap of Morse on pane,
spirits dampened
by barrage bleat of rain
again, and again,
wept pour inane
the bane of tutting washday hangers.

"Ooh, I'll never get my sodding washing dry at this rate!" - Noah's wife (Naamah)

My guess is she was stood by a porthole, hands on hips shaking her head and tutting, a lot! Most likely livid because against her better judgement Noah hadn't included two tumble dryers but had included a double length Scalextric for himself.

I have fact checked The Book of Genesis (Ted Rogers 3:21) and indeed it was a 'TCR,' Total Control Racing Scalextric, that Noah had smuggled aboard his Arc.

They no doubt passed the time running 10 lap races, winner stays on obvs.

Travelling wife

I miss her smile
her slamming doors
I miss her laugh
her mopping floors
I miss her cuddles
her washing up
I miss her chunky
her trail of cups
I miss her love
her tired groans
I miss her touch
her riled tones
I miss her dimples
her piggy snores
I miss her nursing
her doing chores
I miss her joy
her flatulent forces
I miss her lots,
but not the stench of her stinky horses.

I sent this poem, and below message, to Kimsy while she was away working in New Zealand for 7 weeks.

"While our Pans haven't missed you, I have actually missed your culinary delights and the amusement/digestive challenges they bring.

Erm, might I enquire when you will be back from New Zealand please darling as I am running low on clean clothes, and am now on paper plates! Also, my monthly bath is this coming Thursday, did you manage to organise one of your friends to visit and bathe me? I can't do it myself; I will get shampoo in my eyes and be all of a panic. Love you."

2-minute beach clean

Residuals of callous individuals
left scattered, strewn,
spewed all over beaches
confusing local creatures
littering literally at its most lazy
so crazy
how selfish some people can be.
Take it with you
your/you're rubbish
don't leave it by the Sea
for me to have to tidy up!

I'm moving to the seaside, gonna clean a lot of beaches.

Open water

Moonglade glimmer
mesonoxian dipper,
swimmer, cuts coast denticulation,
bathed in deep, serene isolation
an oscillation of sweeping arms
and flutter foot kick,
lapped lick of waves, salted.
Bubbling, cresting, lace chaotic
hypnotic in motion, carried.
Foam parried,
supine in stroke
lulled languid float
in calm of tranquil cove.
Swell in saunter, such delight,
of open water trove.

I would dearly love to be one of those 'brave open water swimmers,' alas, the truth of the matter is that I am way out of my depth just when having a bath!

Oh, and am also very nesh! I love, and respect the open water/sea, but it is way too cold in the UK for outdoor swimming.

Sans Syrup

Give-over, with tha's comb-over,
we all know ya's losing
a battle of dire dissolve.
Your resolve tested, bested
by baron wicket
your thicket sparse, bare
as baboons' arse
and by folly of follicle frailty
austerity of barber trim visits arrive.
Pride, dented by measly mane
such cruelty, such pain
in raked ridiculous villus,
thatch thinning, demeaning prowess
and resulting 'Charlton-esque' crisis.

When I was 11, I did a week at Bobby Charlton's Soccer School. Bobby visited every day and played little 5-a-side games with all the players of all ages. He was amazing, and his persona was something I'd only ever seen before in my own uncle Bob.

Anyways, I 'Megged' Bobby Charlton in one of our 5-a-side games, and I beat him at Table Tennis later the same day. I'll never forget the way he carried himself and how he made time to speak and to help others. Such a wonderful person. Should never have gone with a comb-over though.

'Syrup', aka 'Syrup of Fig' is Cockney Rhyming Slang for a wig.

Hair, bear bunch

A topiary tamed 'do'
rough cut by sword
of Beastie Boy accord
and Joe Dirt award
a head, ahead of trend.
Full send
on track
the business in the front
party in the back.

According to Wikipedia, the term 'Mullet' originated with a 1994 Beastie Boys song called "Mullet Head", while the 2001 movie 'Joe Dirt' gave us the description "The business in the front, party in the back".

Panic room

Days culled
annulled
when caught
in web of doubt
through spiralled thought,
terrifying tiers of fears
evoke tears
of addled, disconcerting discord.
Savaged
mauled
a thousand cuts by demon sword,
onlookers appalled
by inexplicable display of doom.
Oh, why must this curse curate my room.

Sometimes there is just no stopping the terrifying rush of debilitating fear when anxiety kicks in. I usually try to look out for the warning signs and for triggers, but neither helps nor reassures a tired mind. A wandering tired mind is all too easily gobbled up by invisible demons, and a paralysing panic ensues.

Of all the superpowers I could have been blessed with, Anxiety is definitely the one I would not have asked for. 'Anxiety Man' is just not a great Marvel character!

In hope we trust

"Don't follow me, I'm lost"
buzzed the bee to the wasp mid bimble
as simple worker bumble banked
through wicked thicket of prickles!

Barbed bristles teeth bared
seethe speared, feared
by even the most agile airborne squadron,
for spiked curmudgeons of the meadow smite.

"There's hope, there's light" fizzed the wasp
cutting curved canopy climb. Carefully navigating brash vine
in compatriot lead, a togetherness rarely seen
amidst the wilds of nature.

"Laters" hummed the bee.
"Don't be a stranger" quipped the wasp,
*"You know, it is ok to be lost
every now and again."*

From my own experiences I know that there is always 'someone' who can help us find a way to move forward when we are struggling.

I know that we can find solace in unexpected moments if we find the courage to share our thoughts, and talk. That 'someone' can be anyone, you just need to ask.

And I honestly believe that regardless of how lost we might feel sometimes, that there is always hope.

Clowder

Nocturnals' nemesis
prowling terraces
elongated in belly crawled sprawl.
Scaling fences, traversing walls
immune to callousness of fall.
Pawed, their catch no match for torturous play
as clawed community glowers
in scrutiny of rodent remediation.
Sans affiliation to loyalty
as if royalty,
the colluding aloof laze upon roof
self-appeasing
easing through days
basking in rays
ignoring their servants' calls
while they bathe.

Domestic Cats spend approximately 70% of their lives sleeping. When they are not sleeping, they are either out terrorising small rodents/birds or pretending to be affectionate until you feed them.

Dare to be you

Twittering on,
chirped morning chorus rings
like loquacious mums of idle stir
it brings
us all another new day to explore
to enjoy,
and go forth we must
to feel alive
with a lust for life
the wildest ride is ours.
Days
minutes
hours
our prowess
our powers
marvelled flowers
endless skies
our prize, is to exist
as individuals amidst
a mixed collective
of callous types
those with gripes
and those who care,
so just dare to be you
among those who try to drag you down
elope from frown
share the love, and share your smiles,
I am here wishing you the happiest of miles
in your very own magic shoes.

Dream big and be the dream. You can do and be anything you want.

Gist

Fresh
bracing
white horses racing
galloping in.
Wild raging din
swells
tumbling rocks
tossing up shells,
she sells
whence lapped calm returns.

As folklore has it, Mary Anning (a very under-appreciated palaeontologist in her time) inspired the famous tongue-twister "She sells seashells by the seashore."

Mary didn't actually sell seashells by the seashore, but it is Poetic justice that her name was not consigned to the shadows. Instead, her work and accomplishments will be forever remembered thanks to a saying recited over and over around the world. Look her up.

Sales Force

Meal deals
diesel wheels
long lonely roads
peer pressured yields
to pitched spiels
in cold calling
fast talking
product hawking pester.
Across the country to Leicester,
for a two o'clock Service Station stop
and a progress meeting
where obnoxious chatter
irritates those eating!
For punter's eyes despise the guise
of the Sales Force
and their endless smarmy lies.

"Sales is a lot like making love to a beautiful woman..." - Swiss Toni.

Public observer

The watcher, watching.
Gifting new lives to those passing by
comings and goings I know not why
yet coy so as to avoid the focal void
of an awks eye contact corridor.
For young to youth, to yonker
personalities assigned in silent banter
at snails, or trip skip canter
they flit in and out of view,
new subjects appearing for appraisal
upon an ever-scrolling easel
of random Doe dressage.

I love people watching, it is one of my favourite pastimes during my idle moments. These very entertaining moments are usually experienced while waiting for Kimsy to try on a plethora of shoes, or while gallantly shaking my head when asked if the dress she's trying on makes her bum look big. (As if!)

I giggle to myself as I assign careers and lives to those passing me by. All the while being super careful not to stare or make eye contact as I find joy in their choice of clothing, their mannerisms, and sometimes their all too jolly or traipsing gait.

Content that my secret scrutiny doesn't offend them, I am completely unashamed in my silent judgement of the passing performances of auditioning strangers. Next please!

Corduroy

Corduroy,
the hipster's choice
of corrugate joy
a rutted ploy
for girl or boy
the fashion hoy
of student coy
a faux pas toy
of stylist deploy.
Corduroy,
a wale loop loin
of fine line
or elephant employ.

You usually see a Cord on an older bloke, that of a baggy brown jumbo trouser accompanied by a beige cardigan. Or, in a fine wale of emerald green, skintight and half-mast, donned by a wanky student desperately vying to be different.

Bored of the flies

Rainbow ribbons rail my fort from flies
from their annoying central circling glide
from their shitty shoes on cleaned side
and their stupid bumping window sighs.
Open your eyes flies,
just fly out the same way you flew in!

When I was a child, I asked my Dad "Where do all the flies go in Winter?" and he said, "To hide." For years I honestly thought he meant 'Hyde in Stockport...' Perhaps I am just as stupid as said flies.

Nephrologist's muse

Silver lined
fluffy wool
glacier white
dark, dull.
Bilious plumes
wispy waifs
mottled marble
crepuscular breaks.
Blown, angry
hurried shifting
soft silent
graceful drifting.
Moody, moonlit
shadowing shrouds
nephrologist musings
those wondrous clouds.

Up above the streets and houses, more often than not it is usually proper cloudy in Manchester.

Flower power

New brush sweeps clean
Spring's flush to be seen
put scene, that of ebullient accord.
Bumbles aboard, busy, buzzing,
a covering of lusting dusting to sneeze,
away in the breeze
new life breathes.
Perfect petals bode
delightful delicate scrolls
as Eden's rise
idyllic in guise
of watercolour, fuller,
is swished in capture
her rapture in bloom.

I love to see the power and freshness of Spring as it wakes.

Unity

Enhancing her landscape
earth danced into new shapes
shifted
raked
cultivated
caressed.
Slapped,
dressed
impressed by design, dedication, and teamwork.
Such beauty in Unity
the dreamwork of riders Fifty to One.
A growing community lead by those
who inspire generations both young and old.
Those ever grateful for their inspiration,
imagination, and courage to evolve.
For everyone there, truly Loves Back Wheel.

The beautiful (and arduously) sculptured landscape of Unity Woods is that of ultimate pleasure to the rider's eye, and rush to the sender's heart. Such a refreshing place of friendship, team ethic and pure invigorating fun.

Pay and display

We parked in the car park at nearby Tor
to go for an evening stroll across the moor
where, to our surprise
we heard a woman screaming to Derek "FOR MORE!"
And then we saw,
we saw them gathered around a tatty Ford Focus
that was rocking side-to-side with squeak spring chorus.
Doggers! Dogging!
And more than just snogging,
'twas a tad risqué for a pay and display!

According to repeated affirmations from Derek, "Tracey absolutely loved it!"

Concerned, I pushed through the crowd and asked Tracey if she was ok, and if she needed any help. She said, "Yes, my foot is stuck in the steering wheel, and I've lost an earring." It was at that point I knew she was safe, so I left...

Proboscis

No, it doesn't suck up cats
nor party lines by the kilo
it isn't for aerodynamics
like on a dirigible,
it isn't a sail
I don't spin around in the wind
it isn't Roman roaming
it can't open tins,
it doesn't cause panic
when I swim on my back
because it isn't a dorsal
it hasn't ever been tagged,
it didn't grow when I lied
it isn't really that big
and I don't use a shovel
when I'm having a pick,
I'm not Nostril-darmus
I can't foresee an event
and when I lie under the covers
it doesn't look like a tent,
alas I'm never offended
by all that's been said
as I know my cheeky button nose
is just out of proportion with my very small head.

Does size really matter? If it does, I've got a big one...

Quite Frank, Poetry

Of the many, podcasts they are ten a penny.
No, not this one, this one is a world apart
it is from the heart. Enthused with passion
never led by fad nor fashion
a true celebration of the attraction
that which Poetry brings.
You can feel the joy as his heart sings
the hymns, the sonnets, the prose
composed by those he knows
are just that bit different from you and I.
With timeless wisdom, brimmed with pride
he guides. He guides us through
the old the new, each word sold true
to the writer. Analogy sighter,
decipherer, of the mystery and ruse
shared by legislators and prophets
he broods. His muse the muse of poets,
part education, part self-indulgence
and we know it,
we know it means absolutely everything to him.

In his Poetry Podcasts, Frank Skinner lifts the veil from the hidden beauty of the world of Poetry. He decodes poems, educates us, and basks in the celebration of his love for the construed imagination of his favourite Poets.

"Poetry is a mirror which makes beautiful that which is distorted" - Frank ensures said mirror is clean and clear for us all to see. He's proper coolsden is Frank!

Smiggles' regulars

Slide. Click. Go.
A lemon drizzle recipe in faint Yellow.

Goth's choice, Black, for memoirs of despondence.
(Adults use it sensibly for grown-up correspondence).

Birthday cards in Blue, and for shopping list scrawl,
Orange is for doodles of Donald Trump on his wall.

Purple is for people eater sketches and memes,
also used for margin notes in the epistolary of Celies.'

Red for marking homework, or spell checking a partner's diary
Pink for they/them/he/she folks' workings out of binary.

Green the official memo hue of the Lawn Tennis Association,
Smiggles' retracting rainbow pen gifts us true ink improvisation.

"Eight coloured inks at the flick of a switch in one chunky multi-point pen, WHO KNEW! Suddenly, the Bic 4 colour pen seems somewhat inadequate." – Frank Skinner

I honestly cannot believe in Frank Skinners hour of need that 'Smiggle UK' didn't offer up any kind of sponsorship for his Absolute Radio show! A chunky multi-point pen for each member of staff at Absolute Radio would have easily clinched the deal. Sadly, at time of writing, the radio waves are now rather desolate without Frank.

Fridge Fairy

Polycarbonate chilled tomb
a gloomed womb of discontent
carries listless lament of leaking legumes
while whiffed gip of fumes consumes
in doomed drawer of atrophy.
Devoid of empathy
a dire desolate place
of rotten forgotten food, where
rancid rooting potatoes protrude
through mouldy cucumber
and glooped wonder of tired Tomatoes.
Lettuce, museum brown!
Peppers frown, disowned
dishevelled in frailty,
geriatric carrots bendy
mushrooms hairy,
and all so scary, that
a fridge fairy is urgently required within.

Every time we do a big shop we always buy in fresh salad/veg, and I always joke that we "should just throw it all straight in the recycling bin as soon as we get home." Thus, saving the efforts of the 'Fridge Fairy' (the person in your family who takes it upon themselves to clean the fridge) having to clean out the mouldy salad/veg drawer in three weeks' time!

A bag, for life.

That word, "*Cancer!*"
Brings harrowing dread when you hear it said
about you, or someone you love.
It can curdle your soul, swallow you whole
but not Kimsy, wow, she's absolutely incredible!

For her, it was never a dilemma to Stoma.
Nor did she wince at 'Colorectal Coring,'
it was the only way, plus she quipped,
"*It will save me at least
half an hour each morning.*"

And then came the double jeopardy,
Chemotherapy!
A portal line, fragility remind,
how kind, compassionate
and brilliant Dr Hassan, and his wonderful team.

A bag, for life;
a literal trade was made,
and our gratitude can never be fully repaid
for the courage and skills
of Mr Mo Saeed and the heroes who saved her.

My beautiful wife Kimsy was diagnosed with Colorectal Bowel Cancer in February 2024. No one deserves Cancer, especially not Kimsy.

The way Kimsy faced this head on was absolutely incredible! Her positivity, her focus, and her strength of mind rubbed off on all around her. For all the while she was dealing with her own life changing circumstances, she was always thinking of others and encouraging others to get themselves checked. Kimsy was also part of the Alexandra hospital campaign for bowel cancer screening awareness, using her own very unlucky experiences to inspire others to "ignore the taboo of poo," and to "get it checked." I am in awe of Kimsy's courage and pragmatic approach, I couldn't be more proud of her.

Kimsy's courage matched that of the compassion and knowledge of Mr Mo Saeed her Colorectal consultant, Domm her Stoma Care Nurse, all on Chester, and Lancaster wards, Dr Jurjees Hassan her Chemotherapy consultant, Carla, Nicola, Helen, Debbie, and Eamon (the amazing Cancer Care team), and the super NHS

District Nurses. For where would we be without all of these incredible people, I could never ever thank them all enough for saving the life of the one I love. I will be forever in their debt, we all are.

Is my PA on leave?

I cut my finger yesterday,
somehow pricked it on a thorn
the nicked cuticle is so sore,
alas this doesn't compare to what you went through.

I had to bath myself yesterday,
I forgot the bubbles and my duck
I had to chisel away at a tidemark of muck,
alas this doesn't compare to what you went through.

I had to dress myself yesterday,
make my own toast and tea
no one cut it into triangles for me,
alas this doesn't compare to what you went through.

I had to tie my own shoelaces yesterday,
I really struggled, and couldn't make the loop shape
I gave up in the end and just wrapped them with tape,
alas this doesn't compare to what you went through.

I had to do some tidying-up yesterday,
I engaged in an arduous plethora of chores
(mostly feeding pigeons and closing cupboard doors),
alas this doesn't compare to what you went through.

I didn't have any dinner yesterday,
I waited and waited but nothing ever came
the smoke alarm didn't shout, there wasn't blasphemy or flames,
alas this doesn't compare to what you went through.

I had no one to pass me things yesterday,
and despite ringing my Service Bell in utter despair
I had to keep getting up out of my chair,
alas this doesn't compare to what you went through.

I had no one to tuck me in at bedtime yesterday,
cold and forlorn, no one snored me to sleep
and it took me forever to count my own sheep, alas
none of this compares to what you went through yesterday.

My gratitude couldn't ever be repaid to all the kind and truly amazing people who have been involved in helping my beautiful wife Kimsy during her unfortunate illness. I am so grateful for all the messages of support and well wishes she has received, and for the lovely cards and humbling gifts too. Thank you all so much!

All of the staff at The Alexandra Hospital involved in fixing Kimsy have been absolutely incredible. And I really don't want to imagine where would we be without the compassion and skills of Mo Saeed, Jurjees Hassan and their medical teams, they are all truly brilliant, and I will always be grateful for them.

Amazing Angels

Compassionate camaraderie,
thoughtfulness in entirety
throughout every aspect of care
succour and reassurance.

Endurance shared; dignity spared
amid unabated sincerity of smiles.
Vitals, checked over and over
devout in endeavour to comfort and calm.

Sans qualm, of Nightingale appease
a niche band of humanity remains
healing pains of physical and invisible duress,
we thank you, we thank you all for giving us your best.

My wife Kimsy has been through so much worry and pain with her illness, more than enough to topple anyone. Her courage and positivity have been rewarded with the most amazing and compassionate care we could ever have hoped for. Everyone involved in Kimsy's recovery at The Alexandra Hospital has been absolutely incredible, and for their part in saving her life I am eternally grateful.

Thank you so much, you are all 'Amazing Angels.'
– written in a card for the Nurses at The Alexandra Hospital.

Mr Overall

Without outfit
or powder of Geisha
the food much nicer
now that I am cooking after her.
It's not all 'Pot Noodle Barms
and biscuits' though,
as I adhere to apron responsibilities
cuisine possibilities
and the safeguarding of pan identities
by attentive timing of dinner.
At beck and call to bell ringer
avoiding reprimands
meeting her demands
of three nutritious meals
plus regular coffees and cake,
they're shop bought though
as I simply haven't any time to bake
what with doing the washing
and tidying, hoovering and pots!
À la Cinders my shifts are long and arduous
but regardless, I do them because she's beautiful
and obvs because I love her lots.

At some point this year Kimsy and I will both go to the ball. For now though, we shall just dig in and crack on.

(Mr Overall gives reference to 'Mrs Overall' (Julie Walters) the elderly tea lady in Acorn Antiques with Victoria Wood, who believed that all problems could be solved with a nice cup of tea, a macaroon, and an anecdote) - wouldn't that be nice.

Sea me

Buffeting crisp cutting winds glide
gulls in chip steal swoop dared swing.
Brings din of ocean splash and spill,
dudes reap thrill atop white tipped arches.

Tide marches in, encroaching copse
of bather's towels and picnic plots
lace like bubbles surge, in earnest urge
to wipe clean the castles and polish pebbles.

We gorp in awe of breaking bore
vast moving creeping pour,
cliff jutting jaw braces for brash
and crash of swell, as rocky dells disappear.

For lapped shoreline steer of lunar ruse
soothes even the most troubled souls,
as human shoals we contemplate the depths
from whence we came.

Rumour has it we evolved from the sea over 500 million years ago. Not me, no I was found as an infant in a wicker basket floating next to some reeds by a bloke called Moses (who rambled on about a similar thing happening to him).

Turns out his full name was Remi Moses, a lovely fella, and I will never forget him; for he gave me my first football, and for some strange reason advised me to watch my back around Easter.

Puppy love

The deepest cut
a wound so callous
without strike from hate
without melee of malice,
one scythed from love
a love so special
for souls so perfect
for souls so gentle,
unconditional love
of loyalty follow
wrenched heartstrings tug
today, tomorrow.

"It's just a dog" some say, but only because they haven't ever known the special bond and love a dog brings to a family. Dogs are family, actually better than family sometimes...

While that sorrow hurts, it only hurts because their love was pure and true. Thankfully, the memories shared outweigh the hurt, and we will always be grateful for our adventures together.

Rebel Roberts, April 2009 - May 2024. 15 years, 1 month.
Scooby Roberts, April 2009 - July 2023. 14 years, 3 months.

Now with us in spirit, they will always run beside us.

On we go

Pages turn.
Days, weeks, months, they burn,

living life's lessons
we find love is the essence to our existence.

Our bodies wear old in resistance
futile in while of path.

Alas, we age
upon a somewhat sadistic stage. Unscripted,

restricted by our own fears
we seldom act our years.

Souls, they come and go, tears flow,
while accomplishments vary;

some find the challenge of reality scary
lost unto themselves they fade, silently

wilting as unkempt flowers do. Few
warmed by illusions of grandeur

their resentment, their anger, mere excuses
for folding within their own crass ruse in time.

"Woe is me," is the most used excuse for giving up or giving in. We have one unbelievably lucky chance at life, and we must strive to enjoy that chance despite all that is thrown at us.

So, on we go, regardless of problems, torments, or sorrows. Giving up or giving in is not an option.

For what?

All these people,
all going somewhere
all doing something
all soaking in moments
adapting
surviving
thriving
after arriving
through absolute scenes of debacle,
remarkable
unbelievable
how inconceivable this chance
this chaotic dance
of fragile formed existence.
Experience our remittance, but for what?

The reasons for our being here are unexplainable, and even our existence seems utterly ridiculous at times. This therefore spawns the age-old question; How, why, and for what reason are we here?

The only fathomable answer I can come up with so far is that perhaps the next level is a 'Boss level,' and we are all here just training for that. Discuss...

To the end

Life's golden disc averse by mist
makes morning climb, as time moves on
to claim another day from those
who dose in prone lazed waste retreat.

In seat, the impudent idle child scoffs
at wreaked wrinkle furrows of wisdom
and once sable sheen worn to silver.
By greedy hands of time eyes flicker

as the elixir of life is strained, drained
through veil of fortuitous existence
in futile resistance to sequent sands
and inevitable facetious fall.

Despite the fading light we stand tall,
we give our all, in hope our all will be enough.
Our compassion, our kindness, our unwavering love,
perpetuates youth in fated ageing shoes.

Loving, sharing, caring and kindness are the base building blocks of life. Retaining our childlike innocence and learned compassion for others will always ensure we are young inside.

Fruity

One armed
unharmed
charmed
alarmed.
Coin slot
reel stop
jackpot
dropped,
the lot
fed back in
the bandit spins
it wins
each and every time.
There's no crime here
just a gullible fear
the next person to put a quid in
will be quids in.
Hold em all
flashing lights and buzzes
a glutton for nudges
the gambler trudges away
solemn, glum,
mind numb, retreating
sickened by sounds
of the jackpot repeating
for the next lucky fool
tricked by an autonomous tool of profit.

Every pub has a few regulars who take turns to feed seemingly endless funds into a machine designed purely to fleece the inebriated punter, those pent up on 'dropping the jackpot.'

This is a glaringly obvious false economy, that which is seen by all but the gullible fools seduced by the flashing lights and sounds of 'the fruity.'

Fortune Teller

A big daft cheque
exposed to press
six numbers
plus, the bonus, yes!
Champagne drenched
adrenaline zest
a fortuitous turn
amid life's tests.
For way beyond
our wildest dreams
in absolute scenes
we realise what
this actually means;
that we can now just about afford
to put the heating on…

There isn't ever a cost-of-living crisis if you are a Lotto Jackpot winner!

Unfortunately, the Lotto is a Scam as you've more chance of surviving a plane crash, or being eaten by a shark, than you have of actually winning the Lotto Jackpot.

Matey

Soaked ablution
dirigible duck
bubble topped
immersive tub
monkey oooh's
toe dip
hover braced
L sit
back scrub
relaxed slide
liquid bliss
to marked tide.

I love hovering over a piping hot bath like a gymnast in 'L sit' pose on parallel bars, all while dipping my toes in with the accompanying monkey sounds of "oooh, oooh." Then sliding in and relaxing as I melt into the bubbles. Just a shame there's a dirty great big tidemark to scrub once I get out, but then again, I have staff for that.

Super Cub

Flash roll
vermilion!
Soichiro vision
solo or pillion
of single provision
as if Michelangelo commission
we step through,
smiling
in knowing the Ninety
is the ultimate deity of all,
the most sold
and the most reliable transport in the world.

The Honda Cub holds the record for being the single most mass-produced vehicle of any kind in world history, with over 100 million made since 1958. It owes much of its success to its uncomplicated design, extremely low price, and its excellent reliability.

"You meet the nicest people on a Honda."

Class clown

Ridiculous rhymes
of voluminous hypothesis.
Prose for my rose,
my beautiful amanuensis.
Sans prodigious pad
nor whimsical escort,
diaphanous drear
or convoluted consort.
Near nonsense cobbled
in delight of illusion
odd swears for dares
to mouth soap ablution.
Class clown adjudged,
decreed bootless laugh
on preposterous path
this inarticulate affiliate toils.

I was terrible all through school, I just wasn't tuned in to what was being preached and was in no way inclined to appease the self-importance of the smarmy teachers. The only way I could fit in was to mess about, albeit constantly. I lost count of the times I was told that I was a hopeless case and would never amount to anything, their bleating threats all as dreary as their inept curriculum.

The first eight lines of this poem kind of explain that; I don't spend ages writing or thinking about poetry, I just seem to get lost in the illusion and note it down, hopefully never appearing to pad it out with page-fillers. The last two lines are what I was told I would be by teachers at school, and just look at me now, toiling on their said path.

Just because you don't fit into their system, doesn't mean you are a failure. I always tried my best at what made me happy and evolved in my own time.

1 / 10 MUST TRY HARDER!

Paradise found

Carpet cover, fly bother, bee hover,
busy buzzing
among the abundant beauty
of her elegantly sprawled shawl;
the forest floor,
a swanky swathe of bluebells and violets
all dancing and vying for sight of Sun's soar.
In awe, we gaze,
succumbed to serendipitous serenity we praise
idyllic cross-stitch scene
and the delight it brings.
Birds sing,
songs without words
a perched chirr,
proud occur
they captivate and elate their audience,
as noted sequences gift ambience
with tranquil trill sounds,
peacefulness profound
a true paradise found.

Forest floors and meadows in May are a beautiful, picturesque carpet of vibrant colours and serenity. Proud flowers sway on the gentle breeze all while seemingly serenaded by winged warblers. A snippet of true paradise enjoyed by all.

Johns

Flowing dreams
etched by sweat and toil
of winter harsh
of summer boil,
shovelled soil
slapped and shaped
raked and packed
soaked and baked,
sculpted by genius
to be boosted
from minors through seniors,
roots heinous
in forest carved tracks
big sends on John line
Gasser, Canyon, and Road Gaps.
A celebration of imagination
invention, expression, and progression
all built upon solid foundations
by stoic team of John.

Farmer John's Mountain Bike Park in Stockport is an amazing place to ride and offers up excellent value within a superb friendly environment. It is more than just a bike park though, as Big Cafe smiles set a relaxed ambience for riders of all levels, and bring together a community of like-minded individuals who all get on. Send it!

Write you

To write you memories
casting everlasting smiles
exhibiting whiles of moments special,
experiences all rudimental to our being.

As if to be immersed in seeing
our belly laughed giddiness
a juvenile silliness, that which
somehow never faded along the way.

Shared times replay
true happiness invoked
a warming heart stoked
in comforting arms of those we've loved.

Traversing back, we're mitten gloved
as we recollect forest dens
and resurrect park play.
All as if just yesterday, yet betrayed by click of fingers fast.

Time is inevitable. It is insatiable. But by click of fingers, or blink of an eye it's gone!
So lay waste your time as best you can, as there aren't any reruns.

Help the aged

Wrinkles, crinkles
sprinkles of grey
taboo the numbers
never to say.

Slipping by sly
hands of time turn
ruing the waste
of idle days spurned.

Lagging legs weak
aching joints worn
of fag-ash construe
akin to brittle bowed fawn.

The shame of wilt
like that of flower
the loss of edge
of prowess of power.

In grateful twilight
never succumbed to chair
creating scenes
for them to stare.

No rite of passage
on path pursued
by no means a given
these years accrued.

So as I continue on
life's theatre stage
I'll try my best
to never go beige.

Being given the opportunity to grow old and to live a full and complete life is a gift like no other. Growing old is perhaps the greatest privilege and achievement of all.

Supermarket Steve

Morrissey worked the Co-op near me at weekend
where he was always smiling and full of life
all that despite being born a boy,
a boy with a thorn in his side.

Morrissey worked the Co-op near me at weekend
one day shoplifters tried to unite and takeover
but he played it cool and told them all
"To hand it over, hand it over, hand it over."

Morrissey worked the Co-op near me at weekend
a ratty woman came in saying she had ten kids to feed
he blew his quiff and simply said
"Baked beans are on aisle three love, can't you read!"

Morrissey worked the Co-op near me at weekend
where he spent warm summer days outdoors
collecting hundreds of robbed shopping trolleys
from all over Wythenshawe.

Morrissey worked the Co-op near me at weekend
someone told him his girlfriend had an aroma, that was serious.
He said "I know, I know, it's really serious,
but no, I don't want to smell her."

Morrissey worked the Co-op near me at weekend
his green tabard had "Ask me, ask me, ask me" on the front,
and on the back it simply read,
"If it's not on the shelf, then it is gone, but not forever."

Morrissey worked the Co-op near me at weekend
where one of the girls built an amazing, tinned potato display
and the manager was speechless, he didn't know what to say.
So Morrissey said, "Sheila, take a bow love."

Morrissey worked the Co-op near me at weekend
when asked one day why he wore a frown
he told his colleague "He'd had enough of this humdrum town
but not to worry, because William it's really nothing."

Morrissey used to work the Co-op near me at weekend
but it said nothing to him about his life
so quite rightly he left that place,
as he had every right to take his place in the human race;
- such a charming man.

Apparently, Nicola on Till 3 was a right bigmouth, but he loved her.

Christmas Eve

Giddy knickers, worn by all
without call of star, afar from silent night.
Flashing homes with lights so garish bright
tinsel lined, though few abide to believe in him.
Bublé hymn, a festive Pollock; such frolic hoon painted
by moments of sugar lust rush and booze debacle
ensuing panic of inevitable battery scramble
with kids' dancer amble that bit slower than usual
not bedtime refusal, more inquisitive perusal
in hope of glimpse of him,
though elder ruse alludes to banter of Santa
a goading persistence in resistance to magic.
In absolute scenes of stressed frenzy
unlikely elves scurry in last minute assembly
while hidden presents whereabouts
totes vanish from memory
as forced loft reconnaissance convenes
tiptoed so as not to disturb the dreams
of exhausted urchins snuggled tightly in.
Totes knackered, we succumb to sofa sins
of matchmakers and snowballs
profiteroles and dough balls
Baileys, Pringles, and Chocolate Oranges of course
without remorse, we shovel it all in.
With top button freed by greed for belly breathe, we sigh,
smiling in anticipation of tomorrow's joy, and the cries
of, "HE'S BEEN!!"

"Merry Christmas ya filthy animals." – Kevin 'Home Alone.'

Vermin

While in repose the world turns
on invisible axle, gaslit glare shines
like that of Doner gyro,
we take turns in shaving her resources

our forces cut away her landscapes
as crass intolerable vermin we plunder her gifts
greedy hands sweep to sift arrogantly through her nature
totes oblivious to oblivion and self-destructive caper.

Alas, no one ever gets her a card on Mothering Sunday,
that despite her involuntary sacrifice for us all.
Appalled, I despise those all too ignorant to care
for this beautiful place that which we call our home.

The world turns, but the vast majority of people here are ignorant to the mass destruction we cause on a daily basis. It pains me to see animals labelled as 'vermin,' yet humans are those who destroy and pollute more than any other.

I don't like

altercations
misdirection's
society leeching politicians

pronouns, clowns,
(perhaps one in the same)
VAR, it has ruined the game

liver, shivers
greasy fibbers
pollutants dumped into our rivers

the jitters, born of anxious doom
losing time
drunk spinning rooms

legumes, prunes
cigarette plumes
ignorance of those who always presume

wars, sores
muddy floors
militant rebels without a cause

toes stubbed, handshakes snubbed
harrowing memories
of being loofah scrubbed

privet cropping
tree lopping
isle dawdlers food shopping

capricious callousness
parking cameras
the blatant lies of the 'moon landers'

gullible fools
loaners of tools
sticklers following all the rules,

yet all of this just fades to hearsay
compared to the frigging Sunday drivers

who are still out and about on a Monday!

Honestly, the only thing I really don't like is horrible people. The type of people who have absolutely no contributing benefits to society at all, and only exist by leeching off the misery of others. Get in the bin!

Grifter

I spoke briefly with a Cow today.
Not of farmyard ilk,
but a distasteful woman of rude concern
who ranted on about my driving
and that I had a lot to learn!
"Moo." I said, as I turned away
smiling, and thinking top burn lad, top burn.
She followed me and carried on, and on,
you know how they go on, and on!
So, I stopped and said,
"That's not even my car love,
I'm only 12, and I'm riding this here Grifter."
But, maybe I shouldn't have laughed at her,
cos she reared right up on me again!
"F*CKING MEN!" She shrieked!
And from that, dare I say,
I got the gist
that she might be one of them mad feminists!
Oh well,
not often I speak to a Cow I thought, as I grifted on.

Erm, I am not 100% sure this actually ever happened, it could have even been a dream as I am not 12, I am 26.

A journey North

I remember the time
I paraglided into North Korea by mistake!
Quite a big mistake to be honest
as I was on holiday in Towyn at the time!
I was quickly scooped up by eager locals
and paraded aloft through streets in shackles
to be taken to their leader!
It reminded me of a scene from Tarzan
when cannibals found Jane
and they were fashioning to eat her!
The locals didn't have skull necklaces though
so I was pretty confident I wasn't on the menu.
They all had the same haircut though
that and the same apparel, of seventies era.
And just when I thought it couldn't get any weirder
I was introduced to their leader, called Kim!
I panicked, and curtsied out of respect
though straight away it dawned on me
that I should have done a bow,
but too late now to add a bow to a curtsy
as he was already shirty from my remark of
"Oh, 'Kim' is my wife's name too."
And then the mood in the room grew
when he asked if I was a spy!
I flippantly replied
"Me, a spy, no why, what have you been up to?"
I expected a laugh, but it got nothing.
Kim had a face like a slapped arse
"I've seen that look on a Kim before" I mused.
He looked confused,
and at that point I realised
he's definitely a wrongun that Kim-Jong-Un!
So, I made up a story
that my brother was Hans Gruber
and got one of his concubines, 'Nigel,'
to order me an Uber.
It, a horse-drawn-cart, promptly arrived
so I said my goodbyes
and headed off to the airport.
Well, I say airport, it was just a shed in a field,
and I thought my fate to be sealed

when a rickety old biplane of Wright Brothers ilk taxied in!
The grin of the security guard said it all
as when I asked about duty free cigs, he said
"no-at-all-we-have-phuk-all."
I was livid, but not hateful,
just very grateful to be on my way back
to beautiful drizzly Towyn.

Looking back, I was actually very lucky to get out *of North Korea alive. The only time I have ever been that scared before was when Kimsy made me a three-course meal for Valentine's Day. Never again!*

Get real

Living the dream
as happy as the cat
who got the cream.
But,
who even was that cat,
and did that cream actually exist?
Or perhaps it was skimmed away
by a snide Schrödinger apologist!
Ah, the things we've seen
such tangled twist of skein
yet as beautiful as petals rose,
I suppose.

For all we know, our existence could just be that of a dream within a dream. Are we even here?

Mistakes

Unequivocal indignation,
ones failing. Derailing progress
slack sailing, dread against the wind.
Confidence rescinds
unhinged by stutter
in utter detraction from path,
an incoherent nonsensical trap.
Opulent epoch nonchalance, consumed
with ease. To appease oneself
in selfish glut of rut.
Teary glances
rued chances, rude
moments of scathing truth.
Uncouth, harsh memories
of one's very own sewn mistakes.

We all make mistakes, but we should be humble enough to learn from them. That while always ensuring to not make the ones we can't ever come back from.

If ever in doubt, leg it!

Unwanted; the penchant of tension

Often calm and collect on the surface
we are ungracious and anxious,
so restless
the torment is seemingly endless,
invisible demons stalk our subconscious
mind monsters
casually destroy the paint on our canvas
lawless to crisis
remorseless
unscrupulous nemeses to our happiness,
feeding upon sorrow and sadness
stealing our focus
confusing the path of our compass,
without notice we're mindless
feeling so hopeless and worthless,
disastrous and helpless
a tort mess
as a venomous stimulus of emptiness
amplifies our levels of craziness,
thoughts raucous
spiralling out of control into hopelessness,
blinkers of fear forcing blindness
sleepless, the day blurring agony is timeless,
we regress into dullness
breathless,
we know the darkness can't harm us
regardless the starkness of madness it's harmless,
yet it has us,
perpetually lost in its circus
as prisoners,
of our own devoured minds.

The first rule of thought club, always talk about thought club. It is good to talk.

Offended

80s bikes,
they weren't quite
"Gender neutral."
Boys had a Chopper
the Girls a Shopper
it's what society
was used to.
Boys had dens
Girls Wendy Houses
boys wore pants,
girls skirts and blouses.
We didn't know you see
that we could be
offended by the most trivial of things.

Surely as long as you are happy with yourself it shouldn't matter what anyone else thinks of you. Just ignore the inconsiderate senseless sheep, and don't ever encourage them by 'being offended.' Crack on and be yourself.

Dreams of summer

Deckchair estivation elope
soaked,
costumed in cream.
Soporific salute repose
to unopposed drift
of declivitous idle recline.
Bathed in time
in rays
in haze
one's laze
one's only recourse,
of course.

There I was, dreaming of a sunny summer afternoon lounging in the garden with a Cider, and the resulting spiralled torpor ensued.

She/Her

Her commission covered
by blue, stretched canopy canvas
she enchants us
with the ever-changing beauty
of serendipitous, serene scene.
Serenaded as if augmented
by invisible grand conch of creator
explosive in splendour
boomed blooms of grandeur
offer miraculous manufactured perfection.

'Mother Nature' is a personification of nature that focuses on the life-giving and nurturing aspects of nature by embodying it, in the form of a mother. And Some girls' mothers are bigger than other girls' mothers.

Marie de' Medici Cycle

Rubenesque curves
voluptuously teasing
feasting eyes
figures so pleasing.
Exuberance, grandeur
baroque scene
Rubens painted
full figures as seen.
Lustily desired
exaggerated slender
beautiful women
soft and tender.
Sensually sculptured
naturally fine
elegantly sexy
shaped so divine.
Idealisation perturbed
affirmation of beauty
model waifs displaced
by curvaceous booty.

Because 'beautiful' isn't a size.

I love her

She's wild, carefree
the world to me
I love her.
Forgiving and kind
always on my mind
I love her.
Selflessly altruistic
truly majestic
I love her.
She fetches Tea
a part of me
I love her.
Loves our dogs
she rescues frogs
I love her.
Doesn't like my plants
but washes my pants
I love her.
Always burns her hands
a destroyer of pans
I love her.
A Chardonnay Queen
inedible cuisine
I love her.
She loves her horse
'Apache' of course
I love her.
A dreadful Nurse
does nowt but curse
I love her.
A sleepy head
the world is her bed
I love her.
She brightens my day
a crepuscular ray
I love her.
Soft and cuddly
a nuisance on Bubbly
I love her.
A unique vocalist
when she's pished

I love her.
Easy to rile
a beautiful smile
I love her.
Always late
she licks her plate
I love her.
She's only small
never calls me Paul
I love her.
Animal saver
professional dog trainer
I love her.
She works too much
has an untidiness touch
I love her.
Always doing her hair
strewn clothes everywhere
I love her.
Never brings me toast
I dote on her the most
I love her.
A super mum
a lovely bum
I love her.
An amazing wife
my meaning of life
I love her,
she puts up with me
and I am so lucky
to have her.

I love to love, but my baby just wants to ~~dance~~ ride horses.

Crazy Town

She's running hot!
A terse tangled knot,
unpredictable and very difficult to fathom
a tight twisted algorithm of unsolicited change.

Dare I say it, "deranged," even
at times to be a caged heathen
with her game at breaking point
she's silently anointed into gang of crazies.

Somewhat lackadaisical and unbearable
kicking off covers, intolerable of others
lacking mere governance of maddening mood,
alluding to hormonal imbalances so rude.

Stewed, brewed by fermenting frustration
blaming mentality of manic menstruation
on boiled station, with tone elevation she rides
an unprecedented beauty under guise of ghoul.

A la stubborn stool, thankfully it will eventually pass
then, and only then can we ever mention
the apprehension of approach over months previous
as a lucky survivor of her mania and raging rants.

But still, don't ever say her bum looks big in those pants,
for there's no telling when she'll rare up again!
"F*CKING MEN" being her most frequent phrase these days,
so, join with me in warm sarcastic applause; for the Men-o-pause!

"Oh-oh here she comes, watch out boy she'll chew you up" - 'Maneater' Hall and Oates.

What horror

With wide eyes,
we were traumatised by Bright Eyes
terrorised by Piranhas poolside
and daunts of Jaws trolled seasides.
Childhoods scarred,
marred by Myers. Haunted by The Burning's fire
inexplicable fears transpired,
so tired from nightmares of Freddy,
ooh and that bitch Carrie!
We lived in fear that Hellraiser was here
while The Evil Dead tainted our heads,
in Texas, a Chainsaw Massacre.
And what of Rutger the hitched passenger.
Children of the Corn poured scorn on sanity
humanity tested by Jason's Thirteenth Friday.
Childs Play really,
as eerie Fright Nights reigned.
Maimed by bite of a Werewolf in London
Boys Lost, shocked
by Johnny's Shining conundrum
the sinned tension of Seven
jittered jump scares of Alien
and that Psycho, Norman.
Not normal those crypts of Creepshow,
but how we feared for our lives
as Pennywise was IT,
and the Exorcist reaped terror!
"They're here" was uttered
and from what we Saw,
our dreams were never to be the same again.

Of all the horrible characters dreamed up by writers, Reverend Kane singing "God is in his Holy Temple" in Poltergeist 2 is by far the creepiest and scariest thing I have ever seen. No likey at all thank you very much!

Wide awake club

dreading deliberation
taunting stir
mulled contemplation
creak occur

phosphene flares
eigengrau stumbles
torpid, languorous
parasomnia mumbles

toilet slump
piddle tooter
social's scroll
oscitant stupor

rheum eyes
carrot keen
toe stub
bed, unseen

clock glance
exhaustive sigh
nocturnal evolve
dream deprived

"Sleeping is giving in, no matter what the time is" – 'Rebellion (Lies)' Arcade Fire.

Dali's Meadow

Wavering wisps of fleur
blur agin nature's blessèd hum,
depicted as dancers upon surreal canvas
imagination ignites and overwhelms.
Hominal Trees stretch
their far-flung fingers point, toward
colourful Cows and swirling Lambs
as they melt and warp, and wilt
within dreamy realm of Dali.
A peeked district safari
of fantastic, twisted glee,
for me.

Salvador Dali, while dogged by mental health problems, was a unique artist with a seemingly unlimited imagination and endless talent.

The 'Dali Meadow' painting doesn't actually exist. It is just one I imagined he would have painted for me had our paths ever crossed while out and about hooning around the Peak District on our Penny Farthings.

Travelling man

Stuffed metal bird, how
ridiculously absurd.
Choked slithering snakes
in haste, a waste
of my time.
For mine is the known
comforts of home
without wanton sickness
or stresses of journey.
"Return he,
to thy own ceramic throne
for reassuring ponder."

A traveller I certainly am not, for I despise the stresses of holidays and the somewhat baffling need to visit unfamiliar places.

I've no idea why, but unfamiliar places tend to freak me out a bit. Perhaps, above all else it is just that I prefer the comforts, convenience, and reassurances of home.

Snow day

Flurry flown
sheet soft
fluffy.
Languid
yet busy
of free-floating fall,
magical
mesmerising
eiderdown drifting,
thick.
Silenced steps
mere muffled creak
bleak, capped hills daunt in distance.
Shovelled path penance
ploughed grit resistance
decreed abstinence of corner shop visit
that despite exquisite temptation
of cigs and a paper.
Alas, such taunts of Winter's caper.

I always find falling snow to be somewhat mesmerising, magical even. It gifts us with a gentle covering of beautiful pure white icing that glistens in serene silence. It brings idyllic perfection, albeit for a short while, and is such a shame it must melt and turn into horrible dirty slush.

Woman Hitler

A double shot of drama
in toxic tainted glass
an interfering nuisance
so purposefully crass
manipulatively fake
critical and mean
horrid
spiteful
opinionated,
vindictive dragon queen!

'Woman Hitler' is a somewhat fitting anagram of 'Mother-in-law.' Now, while I am incredibly lucky to have the most amazing Mother-in-law, some folks don't! And I do pity those fools!

Struggle

Aimless,
still rooted.
Moments mulled
mooted, even.
Mind eaten
beaten
to lesion, mess.
Oppressed,
a test
without rest
lest, groomed
consumed
when caught.
Malevolent
doomed thought,
remorse
amplified fragility
and inability to cope.
Tattered seams
dreamed screams
lost hope,
begged succour;
oh, to wash one's mind
with soap.

If only it was as easy as washing our tired minds and doomed thoughts out with soap. Perhaps then no one would ever have to struggle.

Telescopic

Tubular,
canned cannon like
bounced mirrored light
delights inquisitive Columbo stare,
a monocular lunar affair
of astronomical exploration.
Star sparkling, enigmatic illumination amidst
a sea of black without a shore
unique in universal appraisal
insatiable, the infinite appetite of Moore.

"I'm sure there must be life elsewhere. We are on an ordinary planet, going around an ordinary star. There is no need to suppose we are unique. We are not." - Sir Patrick Moore.

The Sky at Night is an unfathomable canvas of age-old light and seemingly endless mystery. It boggles the mind to think that the light we see from some stars is thousands of years old and that the star may no longer exist by the time that light reaches us.

0.000002%

Mere particles, in the footnote
of the tiniest of articles,
exaggerated existence
an irrelevance in time.

Meaningless, parasitic
plagiaristic annoyances
fickle disturbances
in grandeur scheme.

Non sequitur to theme
mere quarks of dust upon specks of dust
just, with very little purpose
other than our own absolute delusion.

The average human lifespan varies by region and time period, but as of circa 2024, it is approximately 72 years of age. To compare, the average human lifespan is only a tiny fraction of the age of the Earth, representing less than 0.000002% of the Earth's age. Our exaggerated jumped-up existence is quite pathetic really.

If you think of the entire existence of Earth from the very beginning as 'a calendar year,' us high and mighty humans turned up on the very last day of that calendar year at approximately 23:59. Mind boggling to know that this is where we fit into the timeline.

Revolting

Hatred, envy, rage,
age old emotions
motions from supposed civil society
a sheep like entirety
commanded by the one percent,
those intent on greed
peddling their needs
instigating wars, and
the cause of disillusion among the egalitarians
- those opposed to the totalitarians -
no, they're not all hippies and vegetarians
as the bias media would have you believe,
for naive are those unconcerned
with being free from the authority of others.

'Egalitarian' - believing in or based upon the principle that all people are equal and deserve equal rights and opportunities.

Long before the first civilisations, ancient nomadic groups lived happy egalitarian existences. They talked through their disagreements, never allowing for greed or rage to taint their lives. The only time they would cause harm to another would be if one/a few people caused harm to others within their group, that or if one/some showed signs of greed or dominance. In these instances, the rest of the group would turn on them and kill them quickly, thus ensuring the solidarity of the group was kept free from dominance of a single authority.

Perhaps the egalitarians among us should rise up and take action against the greedy one percent.

Mooning

Winked waining eye of cheese
crescent slung, hung
above our houses, hills, and trees.
Afar, near star,
lonely, lunar, ahh.
A wooed wry smile
of tidal needs
white light it breathes
bleeds sun's glare
reflecting stare
by chance
off of bare expanse
of dust, of crater
pock shone shimmering dance
casting shadows
stretching, ebbing deep
night's creep
half the world asleep,
except for those
chose Nocturnals,
the troubled or the contemplators,
analysers,
resisters of sleep
mooners, mooning
clock watching keep,
cow leap
much peep
steeped in borrowed hours,
with those useless sodding sheep!

'Sleep,' the most precious commodity. While some can sleep anywhere and at any time (on a washing line even), others struggle indefinitely for shut-eye and all while self-internet-diagnosing themselves as 'insomniacs' of course.

Counting sheep never does anything for me. My imagination consistently betrays my need for sleep by conjuring up endless conversations and scenarios, all that which require thorough analysis and understanding.

I blame the designer/creator, as we should have come with an 'off switch' for bedtime, it would have been so much easier...

Night sky

Lowered snuffer
t'other side.

Canvas cover, crept
to endless depths

lest crisp clear waning crescent,
bright. Reflective white

illuminating sparkle
of sequin scatter.

What chance strewn matter
of set shimmering dance.

Lucky glance, to bleached gleamed glare of stare
as scorching lance sears!

Yet all quiet up there
amidst the noir,

without lark
of as much an echo.

The sky at night offers up incredible mystery within such vast serene silence. Yet the seemingly endless view of darkness is sometimes torn by random streaks of light when shooting stars gift the lucky spotter a special moment's wish.

For even in such formidable darkness, there is always light.

Cheshire illuminations

We watched in awe,
aurora pink and green
beam like nothing ever seen
a dream of Northern Light,
oh what a night!

Forget late December back in 1963, oh what a night the 10th of May 2024 was! For it was the unforgettable night Kimsy and I were lucky enough to watch the Northern Lights dancing in the sky above Cheshire!

Beams of pink and green filled the sky, pulsing and glowing in a magical show. It was a dream come true, and all without having to travel to Iceland to see them, which was my dream come true as I despise travelling.

Hoot

Fixed saucer stare, nocturnal study
in shadow lurk, typed heinous hoody.
A Totem topper
familiar to witches, wizards, and warlocks
a stealthy relentless moonlight shopper
in tune with the tiniest movements
and vibrations of the midnight air,
a wise old glare of Athena symbol;
fierce, intelligent, intuitive, beautiful.
Supernatural,
denizen of fairytale realm
depiction of transformation, change and acuity
majestically silent, such subtlety in prey attack.
Yet distinct in lack of remorse for course;
gulp consumed, entombed to pellet of bone and fur.
Without stir, without so much a tear,
relentless in terror, haunting skies.
For through the night, they come and go
the glide of the killer spies all below.

Owls symbolise wisdom, change, transformation, and good luck, but they are also prolific hunters and killers. They terrorise the night skies with their stealthy raids and are the bane of rodents in gathering scurry. The epitome of nature's cruel beauty.

The last days of summer

Stems sway on thermal breeze with ease,
like proud flagpoles of nature their plush petals ripple
their sweet nectar tipple Bee's diligent disport in blossom,
a bumbled bimble random. Pollinating ransom
across blue blazing skies of cloudless wonder.
Without grimace of rain, nor shout of thunder,
where Sun's golden glow gifts warmth to bones
tinting tones of lounged ladies lazed, braised.
Trees fully dressed, impress with best verdant hues
as climbers allude to ocean of green atop branched canopy.
Blessed panoply of scenes fetch frameless meadows
offering dreamy landscapes to bristle of artist brush.
Young lovers blush, lay in fields of gold
their hold, their embrace, aquiver with new emotion.
Such commotion as their laughter reigns,
their smiles contagious in moments to be remembered forever.
Together, as golden embers fade
they play out the last days of Summer.
For seasons move, yet memories and echoes
of heartfelt joy will carry us on, will carry us on.

Summer loving, it happened so fast.

Top shelf

Reality tainting
Dali painting,
through craze
through haze
a spun consciousness
of inebriation delights.
Deferred delusion
confusion
instability
an inability to function,
lay buckled
outside The Junction
unable to even think.
Dressed,
distressed, in pitiful drink.

Drinking, it's not big and it certainly isn't clever...

Antiques Roadshow

"IS IT WORTH OWT"
he shouts,
as he grasps a painting
supposedly from Ceylon.
"Sorry no,
alas this isn't a painting
'tis merely a scribble
that which was hastily done in crude Crayon!"

"I found it in a skip on the way here" he said. That clearly no surprise to the resident expert (Rupert) who, uncontrollably scoffs at the shoddy workmanship of the no doubt 'Nursery School artist.'

"Value," sneers Rupert, "it is sadly not even worth the paper it is scrawled upon! NEXT!"

Wet

Grey dullard sheet
lashed bleat of stair rod reign
blurred pane distorts forked volts
amplified in crashing rumble.

Gushing bubble, indents of overflowing grids
streamed margins eek out carriageway widths
gutters splutter, drains spill,
ill with rushing torrent bore,

such pour. Soaked, drenched,
wretched lousy summer months disowned
weathermen bemoaned in patter, in chatter
we obsess, lest digress because above all else it's always wet!

The average British person spends the equivalent of four and a half months of their life talking about the weather, and one third of the country are talking about the weather at any given time.

Perhaps the barmy weather has us all barmy about the weather!

A summer of discontent

Drab disenchantment
Sun's summer abandon
plans abandoned
good times on hold,
forecast;
to be overcast and cold
projecting Autumn
coat conundrum
humdrum days will blend.
With no end
to window revelations
curt cathartic conversations continue on
about the weather.
*"But it can't rain all the time you know
I promised you I'd hold you and never ever let go,
for there are better times ahead..."*

Come rain or shine, I am always grateful for the chance to share it with those I love.

Dance with me

A night of pure ecstasy
fantasy,
a romance you see
this music to me
a togetherness, so veracious.
Lyrics loquacious
beats contagious,
to bodacious grooves we move,
with nothing to prove
we just love.
Rushed, pushed pulses
gurns obtrusive
compulsive, we dance.
Nodding as the piano loops by.
Arms to the sky, high,
we are one.
On and on we go,
we know
we know each other like no other
smothered in strobes
the lights consume us.
Without fuss
without mither,
higher and higher
we worship the sounds set free to fuel us.
Brothers and sisters
immortal in sample
in our temple, of worship.
Devout dancers for our God, the DJ,
bouncing in unison
a communion
of likeminded dreamers.
Day to night, to day again,
dripping wet with sweat, yet
the music in the house is so soothing,
none stop moving, for hours
passion and love our ultimate powers
these moments ours,
without burden
we are free.
I simply ask you;

to come on,
dance with me
move your body you like the beat.

In the beginning there was Jack, and Jack had a groove. And from this groove came the groove of all grooves. And while one day viciously throwing down on his box, Jack boldly declared, "Let there be HOUSE!" and house music was born.

Rhythm Controll – 'My House' 1987

The painting

Easel stage
blank page
of water or of oil construe
I know not what.
By dream of thumbed unpretentious palette
a banquet of colour
splashes upon an ageless blanket
romantic, even.
Attention given, driven by capture
a rapture of emotion
deep devotion for subject chosen,
such beauty and mystery
amidst the played plethora of colours.
Indeed, perhaps just a simple paint by numbers
but the lovers know it is more than that.
I doth my cap to the artist,
and her patience in painting us.

For Christmas 2023 I had one of our favourite photographs made into a 'paint by numbers' painting for Kimsy to paint. It is of us together, in our favourite place. It will keep her busy while I am doing wheelies in the kitchen.

Dinner for two

Candles dance upon the table
in shimmying shine of wick delight
reflecting light upon her beauty
as if duty the glitter flicker of sparkle
enthuses her diamonds, gracing her smile.

Lush loquacious liquid poured to crystal
winked clink pose pursed whet of whistle
unstoppable bubbles busy in plume
oblivious to goings on in room,
encapsulated completely in her presence.

Her essence, her quaint perfume
in bloom with her majesty
"Such travesty the soup of the day is lentil"
he remarked, as he embarked upon blurred menu haze
his gaze distracted by her giggles.

For starters shrooms of garlic baste,
a taste of steak and chips for mains
ignoring gains of calorific count
apple crumble with piping custard surmounts
to bellies full and fit to burst.

While our thirst not yet quite quenched
we are soaked, drenched, in more giddying bubbly.
As well-versed tributary of conversation flows
she points out the gravy on my nose,
we laugh endlessly, content within each other's happiness.

Obviously not a home-made dinner for two, but if it were, we would still enjoy ourselves, together. For it is always Valentine's Day at our house.

Forever yours

I write you poems
I bring you flowers
I dream about
our love for hours.

I share your laughter
I tempt your rage
I am your clown
your smile my stage.

For on you I dote
your happiness my cause
I am most grateful to be
forever yours.

I don't just love Kimsy because she is beautiful, I love her because she is strong, resilient, thoughtful, and kind. Time changes almost everything, but Kimsy and I remain a constant force together throughout. Together we deal with one thing at a time, while our belief, our hope and our love carries us on.

I am forever grateful for us, and for you my true Valentine.

Written on the occasion of our 30th Valentine's Day, 14th February 2024

Days of wonder

One day,
one day we were young
we were all lay in the sun,
and in my arms
all the things I loved,
it seemed so easy to be me.

At times, our carefree days of youth can seem so long ago. Yet sometimes they also feel like they happened just yesterday. While time is a constant, it somehow tends to speed up or slow down depending upon how we think about it.

Time though, it isn't all we have to cherish. For our memories, and the memories of those before us, will always be remembered forever and passed on through time.

Chai

Bush pick without grieve
mass leave of leaves
from notorious world
(fair trade preferred)
shipped to all corners
and corners of streets
accompanied by dunking treats.
I've often wondered of their final moments;
tossed to Tea Pot
bled to red
boiled to builders
bewildered by a scalding end,
most go unread.

I love a Tea, but I am far too lazy to be bothered with the rigmarole of brewing proper Tea leaves. Though I do often wonder if the rest of the Teabags in the tin think about where the Teabag I've just taken out is off to, and more so, what will happen to it.

I wonder if the Teabags all wait in anticipation of being freed from the tin, only to face the disappointment, and terror, of being lobbed into a cup and drowned in boiling hot water!

Anyone else think that, or is it just me?

Tea and Toast

Reluctant in shadowed eigengrau,
fleece robed
the early rising curmudgeon
trudging creaking boards
to silent applause from pretending sleeper,
she's a keeper that girl.
Crash of cup, of saucer settle
tap splash curse (lid probs still on kettle)
Supine, I hope for normal Tea
and none of that fruit nor nettle nonsense.
Her choice language a constant,
while despondent I wait for charred toast
and stew of auburn strained and bled
as I know the penance of being fed
Tea and Toast in bed at Shepley.

I gracefully receive breakfast in bed every once in a while. Unfortunately though, the standard of cuisine is that of a lowly rated Air B&B and the bedside manner quite questionable at best, yet her beautiful smile always atones for the mess she has left me in the kitchen....

An ode to the modern-day Suffragette

the one who simply doesn't forget
à la Loxodonta, a lexicon
stickle in reminder of historic misdemeanour.
For She, Her, of many mood occur
is loosely loquacious in libation concur,
intrepid in stardom of karaoke slur.
Crude, lewd, Lady Petrol fuelled
does the school run in PJs and a slipper mule.
Opinionated, and rightly so
scrolling through Socials to keep in the know,
yet offended by the smallest of things,
everything, Poetry even.
Some are Ugg wearing, a tad overbearing
while sparing little shame, tact, or common decency.
Rash, unpleasantly brash,
rude in haste manoeuvre of trolly dash!
Alas, thankfully they're not all like that
(*as I gracefully back track rescinding crass views*)
I allude to their rationale, and weeks of calmness,
perhaps so as to avoid the wrath per say
of the modern-day Suffragette
and their celebration of suffrage, for Love Island.

This poem is purely a jibe at 'some' of the current younger generation of 'ladies,' those who are more inclined to vote on the 'Love Island' TV programme than they would in a political election etc.

I mean no detriment to those heroic Suffragettes who fought, and rightly stood up for what they believed in, that which is all so easily taken for granted these days. And I stand by my belief that there wouldn't be any Wars if only women were world leaders, because they would all just slag each other off on social media and there would be no need for innocent people to lose their lives.

Street life

Auto glow
unable to go
still in place,
pace, no.

Male marked
velo parked
hide 'n seek
counter barked.

Tall, towering
flowering light,
daytime dozing
nighttime, bright.

The lonely life of the lamp post, the unsung hero of the streets.

"I play the street life, because there's no place I can go" - 'Street life' The Crusaders.

The Darkness

Ebony canvas diamond twinkle
ebony canvas, pure, simple.

Widow's veil covering eyes
Ra return whence it rise
blanket creep cloaking skies
Apollyon allure, witching guise.

Ebony canvas pure, simple
ebony canvas, infinite easel.

Mysterious mood silenced singers
silver shadows moonlight shimmers
nocturnal nymphs' mischief bringers
expectant air, goosebumps, shivers.

Ebony canvas infinite easel
ebony canvas, righteous, Ezekiel.

"The path of the righteous man is beset on all sides by the inequities of the selfish and the tyranny of evil men. Blessed is he who, in the name of charity and good will, shepherds the weak through the valley of the darkness. For he is truly his brother's keeper and the finder of lost children, and those who lead many to righteousness will shine like the stars for ever" – Jules Winnfield 'Pulp Fiction.'

"Be your best in the darkness or Jules will get you!" - Paul CK Roberts 'Life Fiction.'

The Northern Water

I'm gonna build a Lido in town
it'll fill itself up with all this rain pouring down
sorry mate, no budgie smugglers allowed
Hawaiian shirts are ok though so long as they're loud.

He/She Bikinis, yes they are a must
as topless is a bust for our license to operate.
Sorry ~~mate~~ love,
I said no budgie smugglers allowed!

Don't worry the weather is gonna be sound
but get your tickets early I'm expecting a crowd
and I've got doormen around, jusqu'à la fin
so, if your names not down you're not coming in.

Oh yeah, and it's called 'The Northern Water'
it's two an' half tenths down from The Northern Quarter
and it's for rich or for poorer, but you all ought to
shower before getting in yeah, it's not a bath it's a Lido!

No skinny folks on the top diving boards please as it's a bit windy and I've genuine concerns that you might get blown off into The Arndale!

Oh, and there are "WAVES IN THE BIG POOL!"

New day

Dreams break. Dreamscapes interrupted by first call, a wall of bright-burn hope spurs elope of lunar fade, survivors rest from hunt evade, still in glade they pause to listen, soaked in dew outlined by aurora glow they glisten, idyllic, so serene in scene.

Averse to mowing, the silence of grass growing tempts the blackbirds' busy beaks, their chooking shrieks shrill at sight of pussy prowl laying low among the cowls of foxglove, while wriggling oxblood worms are returned to nested bairns for breakfast.

Squirrels scurry. In twitched tail creep they leap in death-defying daredevil bound, profound in search for dangled treasure, their acrobatic measure of high rope trope is always a pleasure to watch.

Lamppost lined, kerb defined, expectant empty lanes lay in wait for travellers. Miles and miles weaved aisles of Macadam slithers, man-made routes, carved rivers, shallow slots for mechanical swimmers. A plethora of pesky potholes flank thee, road acne, untreated spots, an unease of bitumen disease.

Sans whistle the bubbled boil toil of kettle clicks. Favourites picked to dip, arranged on saucer, careful hands of leaf brew pourer steadied. Chai stirred, red and readied for drop of milk and grateful satisfying slurp of another new day here on planet earth.

Every morning as soon as I open my eyes, I feel that I need to get up else I might miss 'something.'

While I am always grateful for the chance, challenges, and adventures of another new day, I don't ever think I will get my head around the farce which is 'us'!
How are we even spinning through time and space on a spherical rock, whose ridiculous idea was that?

Why, and for what purpose is this happening please?

Chance

She once paused, for flaws
assessed aesthetic incapacities
while her elasticity of smiles
were shaped by poetry and prose.
To chance longevity in comedy,
that nose...
A few pages in (away from the cover)
a lover emerged, and his only concern
was for her happiness.
Galant, chivalrous, of gent occur
his love beamed for her
a Princess he never ever
dreamed of pursuing.
From the start, wooing her heart
stealing her gaze, through
endless days of joy and laughter,
thereafter sunshine and lollipops reigned.
The game played
a family made,
born from love, and rescue.
While she may have chosen him
for his comedy value,
one could argue
that fate chose them both.

It is a known fact that Kimsy didn't really fancy me at first, but who could blame her, I'm not the prettiest. Thankfully Kimsy saw past my outer cover and gave me a chance to steal her heart.

Every day since I remind myself that someone so beautiful (inside and out) actually loves me, and how lucky I am.

Best Man

The best man at our Weddin'
was Michael Lennon,
and I'll never forget
his encouraging words in church.
He said, "Oggy,
WTF are we doing here...!"

The 5th of June 1999, and we were all sat patiently in the pews of St George's church, Stockport. I was calm and collected, and happily taking it all in. The excitement was building, and we were all chatting away having the craic, well that until during a moment of silence when Mike Lennon (my Best Man) blurted out; "Oggy, WTF are we doing here...!"

We paused and looked at each other, under glare from Kimsy's mum Beryl who was sat directly behind us, then proper belly laughed and cried tears of pure joy!

Then, as if perfectly scripted, the Wedding March music kicked in to dowse our giggles. We all stood up, and as I turned and saw the most beautiful Princess in the whole wide world coming towards me, I realised in that moment WTF I was actually doing there; I was there to become the luckiest man in existence, and was buoyed by a feeling in my heart that our love was true and would last for ever.

25 years on from our Wedding Day, and although I am severely malnourished thanks to the challenges and perils of Kimsy's home cuisine, we are as happy as we have ever been. While it's not always sunshine and lollipops, our togetherness has never been stronger. We are our best together, and our love always carries us forward.

Every day I am grateful for the chance to love a beautiful Princess, and every day I am grateful for the chance to share her smiles. Thank you for taking a chance on me.

Poems

I dreamed a dream
of poems, mine.
Freebasing rhymes
augmenting scenes
throughout reams
of vivacious vocabulary delight,
a fictitious flight
of fearless fantasy.
Instinctive, id imaginary
magnificent in moments meld
held by stanza
as if decanter libation
pours elation through realisation of creation.
My situation
my station,
to write and to share
this faired frippery, with you.

I never ever thought I would be someone who writes and shares poetry. I absolutely love writing this nonsense though, and whether you like it or not I am profoundly grateful for the chance to share my words with you.

Epilogue

Through nonsense scribble
I relinquished my English to paper
an account of said caper
in casual bard chisel to rag.
Sans lag, unperturbed
amassed verbs occur
lines purr in gathered gate
to plate up edible words for thought.
In bandage calm
the alms of scrawl envelope me
quietly soothing, smoothing scars
of earth, of sea and stars
a rescue written and laid bare,
shared for all the world to see.

I used to write poetry purely for my own understanding and enjoyment, but sharing my thoughts with others is now a huge part of the fun.

I really appreciate all the amazing messages and comments my poems receive. It is truly humbling to see so many different people enjoying my nonsense, and at times I honestly cannot smile wide enough.

If you get chance, please leave me a review on Amazon, and perhaps follow my adventures on Instagram @OggyM17

Thank you so much for listening, please keep smiling, and always try to be your best.

Love

Oggy
-x-

Printed in Great Britain
by Amazon

50c05ff0-78a8-44a0-9ef1-37e8537944bcR01